The Innkeeper's Wife

And Four Other Dramatic Readings for Christmas

Anne Marie Drew

Abingdon Press

In Memory of Harold W. Drew
1900–1989
"With a gleam of heaven in His eye"

ISBN 0-687-19027-4

MANUFACTURED IN THE UNITED STATES OF AMERICA

CONTENTS

NOTES ON THESE READINGS

Designed for an intergenerational audience, these readings typically require twenty minutes reading time. While the readings might invite theatrical improvisation, they do not demand props or costumes or acting ability. They are meant to be read by a few people standing at lecterns. These readings have been used for Christmas Eve services, but they are equally appropriate for a Sunday school Christmas program. The approach here is not overtly exegetical, nor is it heavily theological; still, the heart-changing message of the Christmas story is central to each reading.

THE INNKEEPER'S WIFE

READERS
NARRATOR
THE INNKEEPER'S WIFE, Rachel
THE INNKEEPER, Benjamin

SETTING
Rachel and the innkeeper are standing at two separate lecterns, placed several feet apart. The narrator sits on a stool, off to Rachel's left.

NARRATOR: The year is A.D. 33, shortly after the resurrection of Jesus Christ. The place is a Bethlehem inn. The innkeeper has just heard some startling news, which he announces to his wife.

INNKEEPER: Rachel, Rachel. The strangest thing just happened. Remember that man who checked in here last night? The one we put up in the north room?

RACHEL: *(irritated)* Sure, I remember. He got mud on the floors with his dirty boots.

INNKEEPER: Well, he's been in Jerusalem these past few months and he told me a story that you have to hear.

RACHEL: *(impatiently)* Listen, Benjamin, I have to go get the rooms ready for the new lodgers. I don't have any time to listen to stories about Jerusalem.

INNKEEPER: The story isn't about Jerusalem. It's about Jesus of Nazareth.

RACHEL: Nazareth! That pathetic little town. I am even less interested in your story now. It's ninety miles from here, and I don't know any Jesus.

INNKEEPER: Think for a minute. *(pause)* Doesn't that name mean anything to you? *(slowly)* Jesus of Nazareth?

RACHEL: No, it does not. But hurry up and tell me what you want to tell me about him so that I can go sweep the floors in the guest rooms.

INNKEEPER: He was condemned as a criminal by the Sanhedrin and crucified and buried. Now this new lodger from Jerusalem tells me that Jesus was raised from the dead. He came back to life. Jesus of Nazareth is the Messiah.

RACHEL: Another Messiah story! I've heard so many of them. Every time I turn around, the Messiah has supposedly arrived. This story has a strange twist though—at least this one was raised from the dead. Now can I go sweep the floors?

INNKEEPER: This is more important than your work. You have got to remember Jesus of Nazareth and his mother, Mary, and his father, Joseph.

RACHEL: *(finally making the connection)* Mary . . . Joseph . . . You don't mean that frightened young couple *(very slowly and reflectively)* . . . but that was over thirty years ago. *(caught up in her memory of that night)* What a terrible time that was and such a strange night when that young couple came into Bethlehem. *(Innkeeper and Rachel briefly step back from lecterns)*

NARRATOR: It is now thirty-three years earlier, the evening of the first Christmas. The place is the same Bethlehem inn. The innkeeper's wife can't keep up with all the guests.

RACHEL: *(in utter frustration)* Benjamin, Benjamin. I am going out of my head with all of these guests. Why did Caesar Augustus decide to have a census taken? He is fifteen hundred miles away in Rome; why should he care about how many people live here? All he wants is more money, more taxes. We don't have any more room.

INNKEEPER: *(sheepishly)* There's a young couple at the door. They need a place to stay. They've come all the way from Nazareth. Can't we put them in the corner of our living quarters or something?

RACHEL: *(in disbelief at his request)* There is no room. We are filled to the ceilings. They'll have to go elsewhere.

INNKEEPER: Look out the window. The wife is so young, and she's about to have a baby. Her husband, Joseph, is so concerned.

RACHEL: *(momentarily softening)* They do look tired. All the way from Nazareth on that old mule? *(harshly)* What fools they must be. Send them away. We have no room.

NARRATOR: The innkeeper sends the young couple away, suggesting that they seek shelter in his stable down the road. About two hours later there is a knock at the inn door.

RACHEL: Not more guests. Ben, see who's there.

INNKEEPER: Rachel, it's a group of shepherds. They want to know where the Messiah is. They say the Messiah was born right here in Bethlehem tonight.

RACHEL: What?

INNKEEPER: An angel came and told them that an infant born in a stable was the long-awaited Messiah.

RACHEL: *(stunned)* A stable? *(pause)* Why, you don't think? . . . Why, no, that young couple was so poor and frightened, that girl could no more be the mother of the Messiah than I could. But the shepherds and the angel . . . Benjamin, let's go down to that stable.

NARRATOR: The innkeeper and his wife accompanied the shepherds down the road until they reached the stable. And there were Mary and Joseph, no longer a weary young couple, but the parents of an adorable baby boy. Rachel was not at all impressed.

RACHEL: That's just another baby. I'm going home. You tell me how a Messiah would be born on a bed of straw with a donkey for an attendant. *(Rachel temporarily retires)*

INNKEEPER: Well, go on home then. I'll stay here for a little while.

NARRATOR: The innkeeper did stay for a long time. At first he just watched. Watched as the shepherds bowed before the baby. He watched in amazement as a glorified host of angels gathered around the stable, and that star—he stared in wonder at that splendid star that had settled above the stable in the night sky. The innkeeper believed that this was indeed the Messiah, this tiny baby born to Mary and Joseph. Suddenly, Ben remembered his wife and knew that she'd be angry if he stayed any longer. After all, the inn was filled to capacity and they were very busy. Reluctantly, Ben left the aura of the stable and trudged home. Upon entering the inn he said to his wife:

INNKEEPER: I believe that baby, whom by the way they named Jesus, is the Messiah.

RACHEL: *(returning to lectern as her husband speaks to her)* I don't believe it. That fool couple has deluded themselves and they certainly have charmed you into believing their story. Let's get some rest; it's already daybreak.

NARRATOR: The innkeeper stopped talking about the Messiah, at least to his wife. He never told her about the three wise men from the East who came looking for Jesus. He never told her how he'd go and visit the baby. He never told her about the long talks he had with Mary and Joseph before they left Bethlehem. He never mentioned Jesus again until over thirty years later when the visitor from

Jerusalem came and told him about the strange crucifixion and resurrection. Then Ben talked again about Jesus of Nazareth.

INNKEEPER: Now, Rachel, you remember Jesus of Nazareth, don't you? And Mary and Joseph?

RACHEL: Certainly, I do. How could I forget how you made a fool of yourself over that boy? I told you he wasn't the Messiah. No Messiah would be born on straw, and no Messiah would die on a cross. I wonder what Mary and Joseph think of their son now?

INNKEEPER: Our lodger from Jerusalem said that Joseph died several years ago but that Mary was at the foot of the cross when Jesus died.

RACHEL: She's a fool. If I remember right, the story was that some angel had told her she'd be the mother of the Messiah. If I had been Mary, I'd have demanded proof. Proof that there would be no pain or risks or suffering involved. I'd want some guarantee that I wouldn't deliver a baby in a stable or have to spend my time at the foot of a cross. Mary should have been smart and told that intruding angel, "No." A simple no would have saved Mary and Joseph a lot of grief. *(She leaves lectern.)*

INNKEEPER: *(directly to audience)* There are too many people who say no to God, but Mary and Joseph were people of faith, who believed in God, loved Him, and were willing to obey. They knew that God's will is accomplished through people. As they appeared here at our door so many years ago, they knew they were instruments of God's plan for the salvation of all people. Their faith was great enough to allow them to accept the will of God.

I wonder if centuries from now people will understand these strange events of God working through humans like Mary and Joseph? *(pauses, leaves lectern, approaches audience)* I wonder what you think of us—the innkeepers who had no room. *(almost as an afterthought, as he prepares to leave)* Do *you* have room in your hearts for Him? Will you say no or . . . yes?

GOLD, FRANKINCENSE, AND DOUBT

READERS
NARRATOR
MELCHIOR
BALTHAZAR

SETTING
As the reading begins, Melchior stands at one podium facing the audience. A second podium stands a few feet away. The narrator sits on a stool to Melchior's right.

NARRATOR: It is shortly before the birth of Christ, and a group of astrologers have gathered to discuss the mysterious star in the sky. Their discussions have not been peaceful.

MELCHIOR: The chaos at this convention is incredible. Nobody can agree on anything. The conservatives are sure it's a star; the liberals swear it's a planetary conjunction. The middle-of-the-roaders pleasantly assume it's a little bit of both. Nobody can agree on the nature of the bright, shining, heavenly object, and we are supposed to reach an agreement. For convenience, we just refer to it as the star, the mysterious star. *(leaning conspiratorially toward audience)* Now I, for one, did not want to come to this convention. I have better things to do with my time than to argue with my fellow astrologers. See, I'm an astrologer; Melchior is my name. The folks around here call me a wise man. Anyone who studies the heavens is supposed to be wise. Well, I knew when I heard about this convention that we'd get into this whole mess, with everybody arguing. Still, people want to know what the star is and what it means.

BALTHAZAR: *(approaches second podium from the background where he has been waiting)* Melchior, will you stop babbling and listen to me.

MELCHIOR: That's Balthazar. He thinks he has it all figured out, this star business. But personally, I think . . .

BALTHAZAR: *(interrupting)* Melchior, you are wasting time. Listen to me.

MELCHIOR: O.K. *(Puts his hands up in disgust)*

BALTHAZAR: Caspar, this other fellow I met, and I think we have an idea about this star. We're not going to attend the convention today. We thought we'd skip the meetings and discuss the true significance of the star.

MELCHIOR: *(with great exasperation)* True significance? Are you trying to be profound or something? What true significance?

BALTHAZAR: Have you ever read the Jewish scriptures?

MELCHIOR: I'm not Jewish. Neither are you. Why should I waste my time on some other religion's holy scripture?

BALTHAZAR: Because as an astrologer, a wise man, you should be aware of the prophecy contained in those scriptures.

MELCHIOR: Do you want to talk about religion or that crazy star?

BALTHAZAR: Caspar and I think the star has a great deal to do with religion.

MELCHIOR: *(losing what patience he has left)* I would have been better off going to the convention meetings. They're all fighting in there, but at least they're sane. How can that star, or whatever it is, have anything to do with religion?

BALTHAZAR: The Jews have believed for centuries that a Messiah would be born who would rule the world.

MELCHIOR: *(curtly)* Is this supposed to be making sense?

BALTHAZAR: The Messiah was to come from Bethlehem. It is written quite clearly: "And you, O Bethlehem, in the land of Judah, are by no means least among the rulers of Judah; for from you shall come a ruler who will govern Israel."

MELCHIOR: Now I am totally confused.

BALTHAZAR: That star has been moving in the direction of Bethlehem for the last three months. Haven't you been watching it and charting its course like the rest of us?

MELCHIOR: Well, yes, but . . .

BALTHAZAR: It has steadily moved westward. I think it is leading toward something or someone . . .

MELCHIOR: *(trying to hide his curiosity)* Leading who? Where?

BALTHAZAR: Well, you're not going to like this, but Caspar and I thought we'd follow that star and see where it leads. See if our hunch is right and the Messiah has been born in Bethlehem.

MELCHIOR: Balthazar, you are insane, and Caspar is no better. You are from two different countries, you just met each other, and now you're ready to take off together to Bethlehem.

BALTHAZAR: We weren't planning on going alone. We thought we'd take you along for company.

MELCHIOR: *(adamantly)* Are you kidding? As soon as this convention is over and we figure out what that star is, I'm going home and that is very far from Bethlehem.

BALTHAZAR: But, I'm telling you, we think we know what the star is. It is heralding the birth of the Messiah.

MELCHIOR: Just suppose you are right, on a long shot. So what if a Jewish Messiah has been born? None of us is Jewish. Why travel hundreds of miles to see a baby born in Bethlehem?

BALTHAZAR: *(almost angrily)* We just can't ignore it. Besides, he is to be the Messiah of all nations, all peoples.

MELCHIOR: *(starts to gather his reading script, as if to leave)* You are talking about a baby. You are a grown man, an important and respected man. Send one of your servants to Bethlehem with a gift if it's so important.

BALTHAZAR: We have to make the journey for ourselves. This birth could change the course of the world. *(Melchior stops rustling papers)* Melchior, you must come.

MELCHIOR: Well, give me a few minutes alone. *(Balthazar temporarily retires, while Melchior directly addresses the audience.)* Do you think I should go? Really, I have so many things to attend to. Even if that star does mean the Messiah has been born, why should I go? He'd still be the Messiah whether I go to Bethlehem or not. And if Balthazar and Caspar are wrong—what a wasted trip! *(pause)* Wouldn't that be a good laugh on them? *(Longer pause, then with mischievous delight)* Hey, maybe I should go just to be there when they see how wrong they are. *(Calling to Balthazar)* Hey, Balthazar.

BALTHAZAR: *(returning to podium)* That was quick.

MELCHIOR: *(firmly)* I've decided to go.

BALTHAZAR: Why?

MELCHIOR: My reasons are my own.

BALTHAZAR: *(without any trace of suspicion)* Well, good. Caspar and I are taking gifts to the baby, something befitting a king. I'll take gold; Caspar will take frankincense. It shouldn't be too hard for you to think of an appropriate gift.

MELCHIOR: *(testily at first)* No. I will not waste my money. If it turns out you're right, I'll just pick up some myrrh or something from a local merchant in Bethlehem. *(Balthazar and Melchior stand silently while the narrator speaks.)*

NARRATOR: The wise men set out for Bethlehem. By following the star, they are able to reach the town in only a few days. No one in the town knows anything about a Messiah.

MELCHIOR: *(in utter disgust, directly to audience)* Am I ever glad I came? Can you see what Bethlehem looks like? I know I'm right. No Messiah in his right mind would be born here. It does seem as if the star has come to rest over this dingy little town, but it has not stopped over any palace. It seems to be hanging over the poorest section of town.

BALTHAZAR: *(to audience)* I must admit I'm worried. No one in town knows of any royal birth; no king has been born. The only exceptional event is a birth in a stable. Some poor young girl delivered a baby boy just as soon as she and her husband arrived in Bethlehem. *(genuinely puzzled; turning to Melchior)* The star seems to be stopped right over that stable. We've come this far; we can go a little further.

MELCHIOR: *(in dejected contempt which turns to bitter sarcasm)* And you were stupid enough to bring a present. Fine, Balthazar. Let's go to the smelly stable. *(Balthazar and Melchior walk away from their podiums, and away from the audience. After a pause that is long enough to make the audience curious, Balthazar returns and speaks directly to the audience.)*

BALTHAZAR: *(at first there is a hint of amusement in his voice, but it cannot last long)* You won't believe where Melchior is. In the stable, on his knees. *(pause)* We skeptically approached the stable, hanging back because we were not too sure of what to do. There were shepherds all over the place. The young girl and her husband were lovingly gazing at an ordinary looking baby boy. While I was still deciding what to do, Melchior rushed into the stable and fell on his knees. He caught the mother rather by surprise. Melchior is there now staring at the child. He seems transfixed. It's as if all his doubt has melted, his skepticism has disappeared. Somehow this little boy transformed Melchior. His life has been changed by the journey. *(Balthazar slowly walks off.)*

NARRATOR: The journey . . . that is often the stumbling block. Not enough people journey to see the Bethlehem babe. Too many people just allow him to be the Messiah without responding . . . without making him the Savior of their lives. I guess it's because he didn't seem like a Messiah. Why even his own people rejected him because he did not fulfill their expectations. But if you don't make the journey of faith, then you don't understand. Melchior became a new man because he believed the baby was the Messiah. Not an earthly king who can change nations, but a Messiah who can change the world because he changes hearts. Not every heart, only the hearts of those willing to believe in him. To some the story of the trip to Bethlehem will be just a wild tale, to some a lovely story . . . but to those who have faith, it is the gospel, the good news. The faithful will be changed. *(pause)* The Messiah is born in a stable. He is God in human form—come to earth to teach us how to live, and love one another.

THE SHEPHERD'S DAUGHTER

READERS
NARRATOR
SARAH
PAPA

SETTING
Sarah and Papa are at two lecterns, spaced several feet apart. The narrator sits on a stool, off to Sarah's right.

SARAH: I don't believe I'm really here. Out in the fields, I mean. It's the first time he's ever let me help keep watch over the sheep. I finally convinced him—and believe me, my father is a hard man to convince—that even girls can tend sheep. My father is such an old grouch.

PAPA: Ah, Sarah, don't be so hard on me. *(to audience)* I am a weary, weary man. My wife died five years ago, leaving me with a half-grown daughter to raise. I am a shepherd, and I have no sons to help me with my sheep. I live in a shack, not a house. Even my God has deserted me. It used to be that I believed God had a plan for me. I thought he was strengthening my faith by sending me hardship. Now I realize how foolish I was to believe that. God does not care about me.

SARAH: Papa, don't say that. Of course God cares about you, about me, about our sheep.

PAPA: *(to Sarah)* Child, when someone cares about me, I know it. I can feel it. *(to audience)* What signs do I have that God cares about me? All I have left is my daughter, and although she loves me, she's too young to understand how I feel. I wake up in the morning and I wonder why I have to go through another day. I force myself to repeat the same routine, same pattern. Nothing changes. I might as well be a dead man. *(to his daughter)* No, Sarah, God does not care about me. . . . I have finally resigned myself to that.

SARAH: What about all the prophets he sent? What about all those God-fearing people we read about? They had hardships, but they believed God cared about them.

PAPA: How can you be so naive? Those prophets! *(with scorn)* Those giants! Huh. One of them gets swallowed by a whale. One of them loses home, money, family and thinks he can talk to the devil. I've long since stopped believing in anything such crazy men can tell me.

SARAH: Papa, don't talk like that. *(to audience)* My father wasn't always this way. He used to be so happy, so filled with faith. Why I remember when I was little, he would tell me stories about the prophets, those same prophets he now says are crazy men. I think when my mother died, he lost faith, lost heart. She had been the surest sign of God's love for him. Papa depended on her and loved her so much. He doesn't even believe God loves him anymore—and he used to be so sure of it. Oh, well—*(to her father)* am I supposed to do anything with the sheep or just stand here?

PAPA: Just keep watch. If any stray animals wander into the flocks or one of the sheep wanders off . . .

SARAH: *(interrupting)* Papa, what's that?

PAPA: *(irritated)* Can't you even pay attention long enough . . . *(stunned)* Sarah, look at the sky.

SARAH: I know, I know. I see it too. Are those angels? Oh I knew you shouldn't have called the holy prophets crazy. We are going to be punished. I am so afraid.

NARRATOR: Now you all know what happens next. You've heard it many times before. But if you don't mind, I'd like to read it once more. From Luke 2:10-14: "An angel of the Lord appeared to them, and the glory of the Lord shone over them. They were terribly afraid, but the angel said to them, 'Don't be afraid! I am here with good news for you, which will bring great joy to all the people. This very day in David's town your Savior was born—Christ the Lord! And this is what will prove it to you: You will find a baby wrapped in clothes and lying in a manger.' Suddenly, a great army of heaven's angels appeared with the angel, singing praise to God: 'Glory to God in the highest heaven, and peace on earth to those with whom he is pleased!' " We've heard this many times, but the shepherds and the daughter were hearing it for the first time.

SARAH: Papa, did you hear that? Those angels said God is pleased with us. He's sent us a savior.

PAPA: But what was that about a manger and the city of David?

SARAH: Why the city of David is Bethlehem, of course. The manger, I don't quite understand. Well, let's go to Bethlehem and see.

PAPA: But, Sarah, what about the sheep? You were so anxious about helping me with them. *(pause)* Well, it's not just the sheep. *(adamantly)* I'm not going to waste my time by going to Bethlehem.

SARAH: In those stories you used to tell me, there's a prophecy in the book of Micah that says the Messiah will come from Bethlehem. This could be the night the prophecy is fulfilled.

PAPA: But in a manger? A prophecy fulfilled in a manger? That's every bit as crazy as being swallowed by a whale. You go on to Bethlehem. I'll stay with the sheep.

SARAH: No, Papa. We'll get someone else to watch the sheep tonight. We are going to the city of David. We are going to Bethlehem.

NARRATOR: So the shepherd and his daughter journeyed to Bethlehem. They had no difficulty finding the stable, but they did have difficulty entering it.

PAPA: We better not disturb them. The baby is only a few hours old. He needs his rest, and that poor mother must be exhausted.

SARAH: She doesn't look tired. Her husband seems so kind, doesn't he? Oh, Papa, he has seen us. He's beckoning to us and she's smiling. They want us to come in.

PAPA: Do you think we should?

SARAH: We have to. We have to.

NARRATOR: The shepherd and his daughter entered the stable. Fear, doubt, uncertainty—all vanished. Sarah knew for certain that this was the Messiah. Yes, a prophecy fulfilled in a manger—and Sarah's father? Well, he can tell you himself.

PAPA: There's no doubt. Walking into the manger was like walking into pure and radiant love. You know I'd told my daughter Sarah that when someone loves me, I know it. Now, I know God loves me. That little baby and his parents are sure signs of love. As I stood there staring at the child I kept hearing the voices of the angels as they sounded when they appeared over our fields. The angels said, "On earth, peace among men with whom he is pleased." With whom he is pleased. What a thought. All my life I believed in an angry God, a God who caused floods, a God who tested prophets, a God who took my wife from me. I never once thought, I never dared to think, that God could be pleased with me. But he is pleased. So pleased that he sent us a savior, his own son to live among us and remain with us forever. Can there be any surer sign of love? God is with me. *(He retires.)*

NARRATOR: The shepherd had an advantage over us: he heard the message, "God is with us," straight from the angels. We've heard the message so many times, it sometimes loses its meaning. But the message is the same for us, as it was to the shepherd and his daughter. God loves us, even though our families are broken by death, despair, and illness. God is with us even in the midst of these very hectic days. And if we momentarily forget, momentarily become weary, all we need do is follow the path of the shepherd and his daughter. With them we can enter into the manger and stand in the presence of pure, radiant love.

GABRIEL'S DILEMMA

READERS
NARRATOR
GABRIEL
THE FATHER
THE SON

SETTING
God the Father and God the Son are standing at two separate lecterns, spaced a few feet apart. A third lectern stands nearby. The narrator sits on a stool, off to God the Father's left.

NARRATOR: The place is heaven. The time is about two thousand years ago. God the Father and God the Son are in the celestial conference room. It is obvious that they are engaged in a serious discussion. Just as the Father is about to speak, the archangel Gabriel bursts into the room.

GABRIEL: *(hurrying to the third lectern)* Hey, you two, we've got some serious trouble.

NARRATOR: Now Gabriel was one to exaggerate, so neither the Father nor the Son got too concerned with this outburst. The Father simply replied:

FATHER: All right, Gabriel, what is it this time?

GABRIEL: Well, some silly angels are up in arms about a ridiculous rumor that is going around. It's so dumb I wasn't even going to trouble you with it, but the talk is really getting out of hand.

FATHER: Gabriel, kindly get to the point. My Son and I are discussing a serious matter, and we haven't much time left.

GABRIEL: That's just it. With all the serious talking you two have been doing lately, everybody knows something is going on; and rumor has it that one of you two is going to be leaving shortly.

SON: One of us is.

GABRIEL: You're kidding. You mean those gossips are right? Where are you going?

SON: Down to earth.

GABRIEL: *(incredulous)* Whatever for?

SON: *(firmly)* They need me.

GABRIEL: *(testily)* Hey, listen, we've wasted enough time and energy on those folks already. Why, the angels are sick and tired of making earthly visitations 'cause nobody pays any attention to them. You sent those people Moses and Abraham and all sorts of prophets. They are a hopeless lot.

SON: They need me.

GABRIEL: Well . . . I guess if anyone can get through to them, you can. *(quickly)* What are you going to do, take over a palace and visit for a week or two?

FATHER: Slow down, Gabriel. We've something to tell you. For thousands of years, I have cared for and loved my people. I have been stern with them. I have been kind to them. Nothing seems to work. They do not get the message. My Son and I have decided that there is one thing we have not tried. We have not yet become one of them.

GABRIEL: *(dumbstruck)* But . . .

FATHER: Now listen, my friend, I created humans in my image and likeness, thinking that they would also behave in my image and likeness. I wanted them to become like me, so I revealed to them what I was. I talked through the prophets and through burning bushes and through disasters, but they haven't been able to understand. Now, I will make them understand. I will send them my Son.

GABRIEL: But you only have one Son. Why waste him on those wretches?

SON: Gabriel, they are not wretches. They are children who need to be shown the way, and I am the Way.

GABRIEL: *(persisting)* But why can't you just go and visit them? Why do you have to become one of them?

SON: Because it is necessary for me to empty myself out for them. I'm going to start from the very beginning as a baby. I'm going to have parents and friends. I am going to be human.

GABRIEL: A baby! This is insanity.

SON: No, Gabriel. It is not. I must become weak and vulnerable. I must become susceptible to human failures. Their fearfulness of God's splendor must turn into loving trust.

GABRIEL: But look at what you're giving up, your home, your friends.

SON: Gabriel, can't you understand? My people need me. They need someone to show them what their humanity is all about, because only if they understand their humanness can they begin to understand God. They need to know that it's all right to laugh, cry, fear, and love. That's really it. I need to show them how to love, both themselves and others.

GABRIEL: *(cynically)* They love themselves well enough.

SON: No, not really. They continually get angry with themselves for their own failings. When they get angry, they think they've done something wrong. When they don't live up to their own expectations, they call themselves failures. Their stubbornness makes them feel like bullies. I need to show them how to be forthright without being harsh, how to be forceful without being ferocious. They need to learn how to yield peacefully to the will of the Father as I am doing by going to earth.

GABRIEL: *(sarcastically)* So the prince of heaven is willfully going to be the king of the earth.

SON: No, no, Gabriel. I am going not as a king but as a servant. The children of the earth don't need a king to rule over them. They have had enough kings and power. No, if the people are going to have a true change of heart, they must encounter someone who is like themselves. I will teach them as their servant. I will show them how to love and serve one another.

GABRIEL: But surely they will recognize your great powers and treat you as a king.

SON: Oh, perhaps at least for a little while, but I have another role besides that of a servant. I must also be their vehicle to salvation. I will suffer and die for them. My suffering will replace their need to suffer under the law of sin. And my death will replace death as they know it, and give them the possibility of life, abundant and eternal. All of this will be theirs when they accept and love me as their Savior.

GABRIEL: But why start out as a helpless infant?

SON: Because a baby is so gentle and they need to learn gentleness. All sorts of people will come to visit me on the night I am born—shepherds and kings. They will all come gently to my birthplace. No brash, boastful people will be at my birth. I will slip quietly into the world.

GABRIEL: Well, I hope they appreciate what you are doing for them.

FATHER: They will. They will. Even if it takes many more thousands of years, one day they will understand that the Word has become flesh. God has been made human. Heaven has come down to earth and eternity has invaded time. They will come to realize how valuable it is to be human because God became human. One day they will learn to empty themselves for one another as my Son is emptying himself for them.

GABRIEL: *(not yet convinced)* You certainly do have faith in them.

FATHER: You're right, Gabriel. I have faith in my Son and in the children I gave life to. Through my Son they will know that I love them, for that is what I have been trying to teach them through the ages, and that is what this baby Jesus will teach them now . . . love.

HEROD'S CHRISTMAS EVE JOURNEY

READERS
HEROD
BALTHAZAR

SETTING
Herod stands at a lectern. A few feet away stands a second lectern.

HEROD: *(matter-of-factly)* I'm Herod, and I am in hell. I don't mind hell; I never could stand those goody-goody types that go to heaven anyway. Righteous people make me nauseated. Hell suits me fine *(long pause)* except on Christmas Eve. On Christmas Eve I always get this visitor from heaven. Balthazar. Remember him? He was one of those three idiot wise men who betrayed me. They were supposed to come back from Bethlehem and tell me exactly where that little baby was—the one who was claiming to be king. Well, Balthazar and his chums never came back to me. It's partly Balthazar's fault that I'm here. I might not have gotten so angry if he had only come back. But as it was, I wanted to kill every baby I saw. When I realized I had been betrayed, I ordered every infant boy slaughtered. That's why I landed here.

BALTHAZAR: *(approaching empty lectern)* Oh, Herod, come now; let's be honest. Your slaughtering all those babies is not the only reason you are in hell.

HEROD: *(surprised; then testily)* Balthazar! Is it time for our trip yet?

BALTHAZAR: Not quite. Go on. Finish talking to the people. I want to hear what else you have to say about yourself.

HEROD: What time do we leave?

BALTHAZAR: *(Improvise a time that synchronizes with service.)*

HEROD: *(to audience with no attempt to conceal his contempt)* This is what's so bad about hell. Every Christmas Eve, this Balthazar character comes to take me on our "journey," as he calls it. I don't have any choice in the matter. It's part of my punishment. I have to revisit Earth—supposedly to prove that I did not kill the Messiah. I hate this trip. I was hoping Balthazar would not show up this year.

BALTHAZAR: You know I have to show up every year until you believe.

HEROD: Believe what? That some fool baby that I couldn't get my hands on was the Messiah? He was no Messiah. This whole trip business is unfair. I don't deserve to be punished continually for one mistake.

BALTHAZAR: Herod, how about some honesty? One mistake? Who are you trying to kid?

HEROD: *(indignantly)* Yes! One mistake. Everybody remembers me only as the nasty old wicked man who killed the babies. Why, I was governor of Galilee, king of Judea. I built a theater, an amphitheater. I even rebuilt the temple. Why doesn't anybody remember the good things about me?

BALTHAZAR: Because your bad outweighs the good. You not only killed helpless infants, you imprisoned and then murdered your wife and mother-in-law. You killed your own sons when you thought they were after your throne. No rebuilt temple can outweigh the evil you let loose. Now let's go. We're almost late.

HEROD: Which sweet little church do you have picked out this year? Is it made out of brick or is it one of those white framed ones?

BALTHAZAR: I've a few surprises for you this year, Herod. Oh I have a church picked out for you all right, but we're making two other stops first.

HEROD: Two?

BALTHAZAR: Yes. The first stop we're making is near your old neighborhood. We're going to the Middle East.

HEROD: *(confused)* We're visiting a church in the Middle East?

BALTHAZAR: No. I told you, I had a few surprises for you this year. Every year before this, I assumed that if I showed you only something good like a church, you'd be convinced that Christ was the Messiah and goodness had triumphed over evil. But somehow that hasn't worked. So this year, I'm going to show you evil too. *(pause)* That's why we've come here *(another pause)* to the Middle East.

HEROD: *(defensively)* What don't you like about the Middle East?

BALTHAZAR: Several people are being held hostage here. They want to be home with their families, but evil holds them here against their will.

HEROD: I've heard about this hostage business. In hell we talk about it every night at dinner. *(pause)* Those hostages don't look happy.

BALTHAZAR: How could they be? It's Christmas Eve. They are thousands of miles away from their families. These people are scared and anxious.

HEROD: Why would you bring me here? This place proves my point. That baby—Jesus, that was his name, wasn't it?—was no Messiah. The Messiah was supposed to make things better, supposed to bring peace. This doesn't look like peace to me. These hostages look like the people I imprisoned thousands of years ago. Some of them have that terrified look my sons had when they knew I wanted to be rid of them. No. Nothing has changed. The world is still the same old misera . . .

BALTHAZAR: *(sharply)* That's enough, Herod. We must move on. We've so much farther to go. Our next stop is the United States.

HEROD: You've never taken me to the United States before. *(almost excited)* Why don't you take me to New York or San Francisco?

BALTHAZAR: Any of those places would probably do, but the church I have picked out is in *(insert name of nearest city)*.*

HEROD: So? The church is stop number three. What happened to the second stop?

BALTHAZAR: I'm getting to that. Since the church we'll visit is in *(name city)*, I thought I'd make the second stop there, too. Oh, we're here now.

HEROD: This? This is the United States? We've stopped in front of* a crummy looking, burned house. From the smell of things, I'd say the fire was a recent one.

BALTHAZAR: Yes, an elderly woman lived here until a few days ago.

HEROD: What happened?

BALTHAZAR: Some teenagers put gasoline around the house next door. When that one burned, it took this one with it.

HEROD: What was the reason?

BALTHAZAR: No real reason. The kids just needed something to do.

HEROD: At least when I did something evil, as you call it, I had a reason. I never did anything senselessly.

**Wherever an asterisk appears, the reading can be adapted to the local church and local current events.*

BALTHAZAR: You're right. This burning is senseless. The people in this neighborhood are scared and haunted too. Just like the hostages in the Middle East.

HEROD: Balthazar, old chum, it seems to me you're not doing your job. You are assigned to take me out on a trip every Christmas Eve to try and convince me that Jesus was really the Messiah. Am I right?

BALTHAZAR: Yes.

HEROD: So far you have shown me grief and terror. Both grief and terror existed when I was alive. If the Messiah had come, he would have changed all that. People would be different. People would be loving and kind. Balthazar, you goofed.

BALTHAZAR: No I haven't, Herod. I've saved the best for last. Come on.

HEROD: Oh, no. Not a church. Oh, I hate this church ritual. Do you know how many churches you've dragged me into?

BALTHAZAR: We have to go to a church every Christmas Eve until you have a change of heart. Once you believe that Jesus was and is the Messiah, we can stop visiting churches. Look at this church. Rather pretty, don't you think?

HEROD: It'll do. It's hard to be impressed. I've seen so many. But I do rather like that little window there.* *(or improvise specific details from the local church)*

BALTHAZAR: Oh? There's another just like it behind you.

HEROD: Hmm. That ceiling* is rather lovely too.

BALTHAZAR: I thought you'd like this church.

HEROD: I don't like the church necessarily. I was admiring the architecture.

BALTHAZAR: Well then, look at the people.

HEROD: They look like your average churchgoing type. *(with bitterness)* There are churchgoing types you know.

BALTHAZAR: Herod, don't be so cynical.

HEROD: No. It's true. I can spot a churchgoer from miles away. Now that I look at these people more closely . . . *(pause)* . . . a few of them are not the regulars. They don't look like they're here very often.

BALTHAZAR: Herod, that hardly matters.

HEROD: It doesn't? I thought good Christians kept records on church attendance.

BALTHAZAR: *(sharply)* Will you stop? What matters is that these people are here tonight, on Christmas Eve. They are celebrating the birth of Jesus, the Messiah.

HEROD: You know as well as I do that they are only here out of habit. Probably some of them have been doing this for twenty years.

BALTHAZAR: Well is that such a bad habit? I mean certainly there are worse habits than going to Christmas Eve services.

HEROD: True. But none of them has anything else to do anyway.

BALTHAZAR: You have to be joking. Half of them are probably serving dinner to twenty people tomorrow. And they don't even have all the food prepared. Some of them don't even have the gifts wrapped or the tree decorated. They have plenty to do. They are here because they believe in Jesus Christ.

HEROD: Oh, I get so tired of hearing that. They only believe because they have never known strife or grief. Have these people ever known the terror of the hostages? Have they ever known the fear of being old and being burned out of their house? They believe in a nice comfortable Messiah because they have never suffered.

BALTHAZAR: Herod, you could not be more wrong. You cannot be human without suffering. There are people here who* have watched their children die. Some of these people have stood by a hospital bed and have watched a person they love perish. Some of these people have faced grave financial difficulties. Some of them have been in and out of the hospital too many times to count, and this church has more than its share of domestic stress. Their problems are many. They have seen evil, but they still believe.

HEROD: Maybe they do have problems, but do they really believe? Does coming to Christmas Eve services take real faith? All they do is sing carols and light candles . . . and collect money.

BALTHAZAR: Yes. This church service evidences real faith. Herod, you did not kill the Messiah; remember he escaped you. The baby born in Bethlehem was the Savior. He is as alive now as he was then.

HEROD: No he is not. I know I did not kill the Messiah. You have reminded me every Christmas Eve for over fifteen hundred years, but these people killed the Messiah.

BALTHAZAR: Herod!

HEROD: I mean it. Look at them. They are sitting here, singing carols, and there is a world of evil around them. If they really believed, they would have changed the world. If the Messiah was still alive, the world would be ablaze with his glory. He'd be enthroned on a . . .

BALTHAZAR: Herod . . .

HEROD: *(with self-righteous fury)* I know I am right. The birth of that baby in Bethlehem was supposed to be a monumental event. So monumental that the world dates time from his birth, so monumental that I am not remembered as the man who rebuilt the temple but as the man who killed babies. But if the event was truly so monumental, so heart-changing, the world would be different. No, Balthazar, you have not convinced me this year.

BALTHAZAR: But, Herod, I showed you the terror in the Middle East, the fear in a United States city, and *then* the church. Didn't it make you realize that even in the midst of great evil, good can exist? That the Messiah is present in the world, in the hearts of these people *(gestures toward audience)* even though there is great strife?

HEROD: No. What I see is that in the middle of great evil there exists an even greater evil. People who have been duped into believing that the Messiah lives. I tell you, no Messiah would tolerate the world, the filthy wretched world as it is today. No your strategy did not work, Balthazar. I've taken my punishment for one more year, but I still do not believe in a living, loving Savior. *(pause)* Take me back to hell.

BALTHAZAR: *(pause; then wearily)* You already are back in hell, Herod. As soon as you said that you still do not believe in the Messiah, as soon as those words came out of your mouth, you returned to hell. But there's something I wanted to tell you. The presence of evil does not negate the presence of good or the power of Christ. There are people like you, the cynics who never understand, never believe. We *(indicating audience)* believe because we've experienced Christ in our hearts. We know the power he has for our lives. The kingdom of God is not dependent upon universal belief, but because we believe that Christ is the Messiah, the kingdom has come for us. On the night Jesus Christ was born, he came only to a few people. Some shepherds, a few wise men, a humble mother and father. He came as a small baby, a member of a family. Jesus the baby and Jesus the man convert hearts one at a time. He may not have reached you, Herod, but he has reached us *(with direct look at audience)* and for that overreaching love we can be most grateful this Christmas Eve.